YORKSHIRE

FOLK TALES FOR CHILDREN

YORKSHIRE

FOLK TALES FOR CHILDREN

CARMEL PAGE

The History Press

To

mi three Yorkshire lads,
tha's legend!

First published 2018

The History Press
The Mill, Brimscombe Port
Stroud, Gloucestershire, GL5 2QG
www.thehistorypress.co.uk

British Library Cataloguing in Publication Data.
A catalogue record for this book is available from the British Library.

ISBN 978 0 7509 8765 3

Typesetting and origination by The History Press
Printed and bound in Great Britain by TJ Books Ltd, Padstow, Cornwall

Contents

Ay Up!

I'm reet chuffed tha's chosen mi book t' read.

Yorkshire is a vast and beautiful region of England with a very distinctive accent. Lots of people visit Yorkshire on holiday to see the Yorkshire Dales, the Moors, the busy cities and the stunning coastline. Many people like it so much they want to stay.

Long ago Celts, Romans, Anglo-Saxons, Vikings and Normans all visited Yorkshire. They also decided to stay and their stories stayed with them. Over time their tales have mingled with local legends and have been influenced by the Yorkshire landscape. Yorkshire's brave and adventurous, and fun-loving people have been written into the stories too.

This book contains a picture of Yorkshire, a taste of Yorkshire food and some of Yorkshire's oldest stories. But be warned, once you enter the land of Yorkshire folk tales you might not want to leave it.

About
the Author

Carmel Page is a Southerner by birth, but she has lived in Sheffield so long that she now uses her back-door as her front-door and has started eating her dinner at lunchtime.

Carmel and her family have a terraced house on the edge of the city, but she tends to live in a world of her own. When she wakes up in the morning her head is so full of stories that she likes to lie in bed for a long time and think about them.

Some days, Carmel gets up early to go to Weston Park Museum where she teaches school children about Ancient Egyptian embalming and mummification. She is very good at demonstrating the bit where the brains are pulled out through the nose. (Not her nose … not the children's noses either! She uses a big doll for this.)

Yorkshire Sculpture Park is another place Carmel often visits; here she teaches children how to make placards and hold demos. She also gets them to spot toilets in trees and paint with mud.

Sheffield has a storytelling club called The Story Forge, which Carmel co-runs. When she is not at her club she is normally telling people stories, drawing pictures or performing with Flying Teddy Bears. She has enjoyed writing and illustrating this book and hopes you will enjoy reading it.

'Ta Luv, tha's Bin Grand'

I would like to say this to:
Kevin, for early morning tea and life-long tolerance;
Beth Guiver, my Fairy Godmother, for so
much more than a big bag of books;
My Feral Friends and the Story Forgers
of Sheffield who have listened lots;
Nicola Guy, for endless answers to elongated emails;
Alex, Harrison, Nighat, Needa and Chelsea, for
sharing their expertise in English literature
and
Ursula and Rhoda, for just being friends.

1

Brigg the Dragon

Brigg the Dragon had breath which smelt of smoke and roast beef.

Billy Biter sat on the roof of his aunt's house. The smell made Billy feel both sick and hungry at the same time. He watched Brigg resting in the fields below.

'Perhaps we will get food tomorrow,' Billy whispered to Tom Puss as he stroked his cat's warm body and moved closer to the warm chimney pot. 'Perhaps Aunt Hepzibah will let us back into the house tomorrow.'

'Meow,' said Tom Puss, snuggling closer to Billy.

The dragon slept in the Vale of Pickering. His wings were arched across the fields like giant barns, but there were no animals needing shelter. He had just eaten the last of the cows.

Billy looked down at Brigg the Dragon. Brigg's spiky body lay twisted across the farmland like a winding road of sharp teeth.

That night Billy dreamt that he had walked down Brigg's spine to somewhere much safer.

The next day, Aunt Hepzibah sent Billy to a cottage in Hunmanby to deliver some new clothes she had made.

'And don't tha drop them in puddles,' she shouted after him, 'or there'll be nowt for thi tea when tha gets home.'

Billy and Tom Puss set off with the parcel. They weren't worried about puddles. The dragon's breath had dried up all of the puddles around Hunmanby; even the pond was empty. It looked like an earthenware bowl, like everyone's empty food bowls. The dragon had eaten almost everything. Even if Aunt Hepzibah let them in the house she was unlikely to have any food.

'Come in and have a rest, Billy Biter,' said the cottager when they arrived in Hunmanby. She looked warily at the sky in case Brigg was near, then she shut the door quickly. Billy sat on a kitchen chair and Tom Puss leapt onto his lap.

'I'm baking some bread with t'last of mi flour. When it is ready tha must tek some home to your aunt,' the cottager said.

'Thank you.'

Billy hoped his aunt would be pleased enough to let him have some of the bread.

'Meow,' said Tom Puss, licking his lips.

Before they set off home the cottager also gave Billy a pile of firewood. She tied it onto his back.

When Billy and Tom Puss passed Mrs Greenaway's home they smelt something so wonderful they stopped in the road. It was ginger and spice and sweetness. Mrs Greenaway was baking Yorkshire parkin. Of all the women who baked parkin, Mrs Greenaway's was always the stickiest and the spiciest and the sweetest.

'Mmm,' Billy murmured as he smelt it.

Mrs Greenaway heard him.

'If you give me that loaf of bread, Billy Biter,' she said, 'I will give you three pieces of parkin: one for you, one for Tom Puss and one for Aunt Hepzibah.'

'Meow, Meow,' said Tom Puss before Billy could say anything.

They stayed a while, talking to Mrs Greenaway about the dragon. By the time they set off for home, with the three large pieces of parkin, it was getting late. A sea fret had covered the land in cold mist. The air was damp and the road was dark. Billy and Tom Puss got confused.

'Is it this way?' Billy asked Tom Puss. As he turned around he tumbled right over his cat and they both rolled arsey-versey into the field where Brigg the Dragon was resting. They landed on Brigg's face. If his mouth had been open they would have landed inside it.

'Rarrrr,' Brigg roared. 'Thaaat's my eye you've just poked yourr sticks into.' The roar of his scalding breath was so loud and putrid it nearly killed them both. Brigg rubbed his sore eye with the tip of his wing, 'I waaant to look at you beforrre I eat you.'

Billy was shaking so much he dropped one of the pieces of parkin. Immediately Brigg's fiery tongue came out of his mouth and licked up the parkin. It was very sweet and very spicy and very sticky, and it got stuck in the dragon's teeth. He couldn't swallow it down and had to suck it like a sweet, but it tasted good.

'Whaaat do you call thisss?' he growled.

But whilst he had been distracted by the sticky parkin, Billy and Tom Puss had turned away, rushed out of the field and run back down the lane before they could be caught.

When they got home, Aunt Hepzibah was asleep in her chair by the fireside. Billy untied the firewood, then started to unwrap the parkin. The smell of the sweet, sticky parkin woke her up.

'What's tha' smell?' she asked as she took some parkin.

'It's Mrs Greenaway's parkin.'

'MRS GREENAWAY'S PARKIN!' she shouted, throwing it onto the floor and stamping on it. 'I don't need Mrs Greenaway making parkin for me! I can make better parkin than Mrs Greenaway. I'll show her how t' make parkin!' She leapt from her chair and began spooning syrup into a big pan. It slid slowly from her spoon in golden strings.

'Get out of my way.'

Billy and Tom Puss had already gone. They knew better than to stay indoors when Aunt Hepzibah was baking.

'Another night sleeping on the roof,' said Billy as he picked up Tom Puss, but he was grinning. They still had a large piece of Mrs Greenaway's parkin to share between them. Soon their tummies were full and the chimney pot was warm because Aunt Hepzibah had stoked up the fire to bake her parkin. But Billy and Tom Puss did not sleep well. All night they heard the clanking of baking tins and the clattering of spoons as the hot butter, treacle and syrup was stirred into the flour and then the oatmeal and spices were mixed in.

By the morning Aunt Hepzibah had baked the biggest parkin either of them had ever seen. It was cooling on the table and nearly covered it. She put on her coat and shoes in a mad hurry, not even bothering to do them up.

'I'll show thi! I'll show thi!' Aunt Hepzibah muttered under her breath as she set off down the road towards Mrs Greenaway's house. She was halfway there, struggling with the huge parkin in her arms, when she tripped over her shoelaces and fell arsey-versey into the field where the dragon lay. He had just opened his mouth to give an early morning yawn and Aunt Hepzibah tumbled inside. The dragon swallowed her up in one mouthful and then made a large and smoky burp.

'Thaaat was a surpr…' but before Brigg the Dragon could finish what he was saying he had a second surprise. A giant-sized Yorkshire parkin rolled right into his open mouth. He was delighted, but it was such a huge piece of parkin that it stuck his teeth together and he could hardly snort. He thrashed his head about; he couldn't unstick the parkin from his teeth. He stood up, beat his wings and took off, up into the air. He needed a drink or he would choke.

When the local people heard the beat of Brigg's wings, they all came out of their houses to see if he was leaving. The dragon flew to the cliffs above Filey. The townspeople watched him from the beach.

Billy picked Tom Puss up and ran down to the beach too. Then, with a huge flap of his wings, Brigg the Dragon threw himself down into the sea, he was hoping a drink of seawater would clear his throat. He was so big that as he flopped into the sea it made the tide go out in Filey Bay and so he couldn't get a drink. The townspeople all ran down the beach towards him, and while the dragon lay gasping for breath they all hit him hard on the nose.

Then everyone saw the tide about to rush back in again. The townspeople didn't have time to run all the way back up the beach and feared they would be drowned.

'Climb on his back,' Billy shouted, leaping up and pulling others up behind him.

Everyone got onto the dragon just before the waves returned with a gigantic splash.

'Hold onto his spines!'

If they hadn't held on they would have been washed away by the powerful waves spraying around them. Everyone was covered in seawater, but they were all safe.

'Meow!' said Tom Puss, shaking his fur dry.

The townspeople started to run back to the beach along Brigg's body, terrified that he would rise up and throw them all into the sea. Billy Biter didn't run. He could feel that the dragon lay completely still beneath him and he was sure that he would never move again.

From the dragon's shoulders Billy could see all of Filey Bay and right along the coast to Flamborough Head. He had not realised before what a beautiful place Filey was. Billy picked up Tom Puss and they walked slowly back to shore. It was very pleasant walking along the spine of the dragon with waves crashing against it and throwing spray into the air.

'I think we should come walking here again,' he said to Tom Puss. 'It feels like walking on the sea.'

'Meow,' Tom Puss agreed.

From that day to this the dragon has never moved. It is hundreds of years since he choked on a sticky piece of Yorkshire parkin and drowned in Filey Bay, but his body is still there stretching from the end of the cliffs far, far out to sea. Over the years the spines on his back have been worn down by the waves. Nowadays, many local people don't know how there came to be a walkway right out into the sea, but they all call it the Filey Brigg.

If you go to Filey Bay at low tide, you can walk along Brigg's skeleton, far out to sea. But as the tide comes in be careful! The sea crashes against Brigg making a loud roar and huge waves spray up into the air, just like the smoke of a dragon's breath.

Yorkshire Parkin

Parkin is a Yorkshire cake made in the autumn; its ingredients include oatmeal. Oats are only grown up north. It is sweet and spicy, but be warned, it might stick your teeth together!

Ingredients

100g softened butter
100g soft dark brown sugar
50g black treacle
200g golden syrup
100g oatmeal
100g self-raising flour
1 tsp baking powder
3 tsp ginger
1 tsp mixed spice
2 eggs

1. Grease and line a 20cm square cake tin.
2. Set the oven to 140°C, 120°C for a fan oven, or gas mark 1.
3. Gently melt the butter, sugar, treacle and syrup in a pan but do not let it boil.
4. Sieve the flour into a bowl, and mix in the oatmeal, ginger and mixed spice.
5. Pour in the melted mixture and stir it all together.

6. Beat the eggs and then mix those in too.
7. Pour the mixture into the cake tin and bake for one hour and fifteen minutes.
8. After this time, test it by pushing a skewer into the cake. If it comes out clean the cake is ready; if not, leave it a little longer.
9. Allow the cake to cool in the baking tin a little while before removing.

If you can manage to wait, keep it for a few days before eating so that the flavour and stickiness develop.

2

Jolly Jocunda

Once upon a time there was a young woman called Jocunda. She did not like doing what she was told.

Her mother said, 'Jocunda, you must not go out on your own! It is not appropriate behaviour for a young woman.'

Her father said, 'Jocunda, you must not drink my brandy! It is not a suitable drink for a young woman.'

Jocunda said, 'I'm going out!' but she just said it very quietly to herself. She did not want to get into any more trouble. She loved her parents but wanted to make her own decisions. Now that she was a grown-up she wanted to be treated like an adult.

That night, when her parents were in bed, Jocunda tiptoed out of her house and away. The streets in York were narrow and full of shadows from overhanging buildings. Jocunda slipped from shadow to shadow across the town to a tavern. Once she was there, Jocunda stood in the light of the bar and she sang.

Jocunda sang so beautifully that people bought her drinks. Once Jocunda had had a few drinks she sang louder and she started to dance. Because the people in the tavern liked to hear her singing and to see her dancing they bought her more drinks. Once Jocunda had had a few more drinks she started to sing funny songs which had rude words. Because people in the tavern liked to hear her funny songs they bought her more drinks.

By the end of the evening Jocunda had had so much to drink that she sang songs with very, very rude words and everyone called her Jolly Jocunda.

Eventually, the tavern was closed for the night and Jocunda set off home. Poor Jocunda, she had had so much to drink that she couldn't remember how to get home. Jocunda almost fell into the doorway of St Mary's Abbey. She leant against the stone wall and managed to walk a few steps further up the street, then she collapsed into the doorway of St Leonard's Priory, which was next door.

The night was not too cold and, even though the doorstep was hard, Jocunda slept well. She dreamt of singing and dancing.

A few hours later the nuns of St Mary's Abbey and the nuns of St Leonard's Priory woke up. They went to their separate chapels to sing Matins, their early morning prayers. The two houses of nuns never spoke to each other; they had fallen out many years ago. Later that morning, after singing the Prime prayers, one of the nuns from St Leonard's Priory discovered Jocunda lying on the doorstep.

Jocunda was singing quietly in her sleep and dreaming about dancing in the tavern. She was singing a song with very rude words. Because the nun who found her did not know any rude words she thought Jocunda must be singing in Latin and so she thought that she must be very religious. The nun assumed that Jocunda had come to St Leonard's Priory to join them.

By the time that Jocunda was fully awake and sober, she had been given a black habit to wear, been welcomed into the House of God and she had become a nun! Jocunda was shocked to find herself living in a nunnery. The rules were very strict; she had to get up very early every morning and sing prayers in the chapel. Fortunately, she loved singing and she sang beautifully, the other nuns were soon calling her Jolly Jocunda because her singing voice was very jolly.

Jocunda found it strange sharing a bedroom with many other nuns and sleeping on a hard straw pallet. She also found it hard having to get up in the night to sing prayers, but it was lovely to be able to sing with the other nuns so many times every day. Jocunda's favourite song was '*In dulci jubilo*', *a* hymn about singing when you are happy.

Jocunda was treated exactly the same as the other nuns and she thought that was fair. They were all given lots of ale to drink and sometimes they had wine with their dinner. That made her happy too.

St Leonard's Priory had a hospital where the nuns cared for old people who were dying and for little children who were orphans.

Jocunda had never looked after anyone before; she sang to the old people and to the children and they all loved her.

Sometimes Jocunda wondered about going home to her parents, but she thought they would be very cross with her for staying away so long. Soon she settled into the routine. It was a bit boring and she was not allowed to talk between breakfast and her evening meal, but she remained jolly.

Then, one day, whilst Jocunda was feeding the hens in the priory garden she heard singing in the street. It was one of her favourite songs and she started to dance. Her feet danced her out of the priory garden and away up the road back to the tavern.

It was the annual Lammas Fair when people came to York from far away and everyone got dressed up in funny costumes and celebrated the summer.

Jocunda had always loved Lammas Fair. Back in the tavern she started to sing.

Jocunda sang so beautifully that people bought her drinks. Once Jocunda had had a few drinks she sang louder and then she started to dance. Because the people in the tavern liked to hear her singing and to see her dancing they bought her more drinks. Once Jocunda had had a few more drinks she started to sing funny songs which had rude words. Because Jocunda was wearing a nun's habit people thought the rude songs were even funnier than usual. Jocunda had so much to drink that she sang songs with very, very rude words and everyone called her Jolly Jocunda.

When Jocunda had had enough of singing in the tavern she decided to see what was happening outside. There was a funfair and she wanted to watch, but the only place she could find to sit was on a swing-boat. When she sat on it, it went down. Two girls saw her on the swing-boat and decided to have some fun. They climbed in too and pulled their rope, which sent Jocunda swinging up into the air. Jocunda loved the sensation of flying through the air and so she stood up and started to sing again.

'*In dulci jubilo*, up, up, up we go.'

Just then, two other nuns who had been out on important business, spotted Jocunda on the swing-boat. They were horrified to see a nun singing on a swing-boat with the skirt of her habit flying up in the air. As the swing-boat came down they pulled her off.

'What are you doing?' they shouted.

'I was singing, *In dulci jubilo*, up, up, up we go.'

The nuns were very shocked and told Jocunda to go straight back to the priory. Jocunda was so drunk that she could not walk and they had to borrow a wheelbarrow to cart her back in.

The prioress was informed of Jocunda's behaviour.

'What have you been doing?' she demanded.

Jocunda had had so much to drink that she didn't remember how to behave in the priory. She started singing a song with very rude words.

The prioress knew what the words meant and she was very shocked that such rude words were being sung in the House of God. She decided on the severest of punishments.

'We must wall this errant sister in. Then let it be God who decides her fate.'

So Jocunda was carried down all the steps. '*In dulci jubilo*, down, down, down we go,' she sang. She realised something serious was happening but she didn't understand what.

The nuns laid Jocunda on the floor by the cellar wall and some of them started mixing mortar. Others went to get bricks. Soon they were building a wall around her. The prioress wondered if she had been a bit harsh in her punishment. She sent to the kitchen for a fresh loaf of bread and a jug of water for Jocunda. Then the nuns prayed to God, asking him to decide her fate.

When Jocunda awoke from her drunken slumber she was in darkness and could hardly remember being walled in.

She reached out with her hands to feel where she was. As she pushed against one of the walls some old bricks became loose and the crumbling mortar gave way. Jocunda fell into a cellar, but it was not the St Leonard's cellar. She had been walled up by the wall that was next to St Mary's Abbey and now she was in the cellar of St Mary's.

Jocunda went up the stairs and found herself in a different nunnery. The women wore habits just like hers and were all walking in the same direction so she followed them. When they got to the chapel they began to sing their prayers and Jocunda joined in. She enjoyed the singing and a few of the nuns looked at her because she had such a sweet and jolly voice. They were not surprised to see a new nun because nuns joined the abbey all the time.

At dinner time she followed them to the room where they ate and she sat at the table with everyone else. The food was not as good as in St Leonard's, but she was hungry so she was pleased to have it. After dinner she thought that they would be allowed to talk and might ask her difficult questions, but these nuns were silent day and night.

Jocunda soon settled down to life in St Mary's and she realised she was lucky to have survived her punishment. She didn't like being silent all day, but it made singing feel even more special. It was a hard life but not an unhappy one, although the abbey didn't have a hospital and she missed caring for people.

After a year in St Mary's, the cellarer nun, who was responsible for all of the food and drink stored in the cellars, became ill. Jocunda was given her job. She had not been back into the cellars since the day she was walled in, but she lit a candle and went down the steps. The air held the rich smell of cheeses and wine. In the glow of the candlelight she saw the glint of metal. It was the hoops around barrels of wine.

Jocunda realised she had not had a proper drink for a year and decided to have just a little drink of wine …

That evening, when the nuns of St Mary's Abbey sat down for their dinner, there was nothing to drink on the table. The abbess sent a nun down to the cellar to see if Jocunda needed help. Soon the nun came back and reported that a barrel of wine had been opened and Jocunda was lying on the floor singing. The abbess went to investigate.

'What are you doing?' she asked Jocunda.

Jocunda had had so much to drink that she didn't remember how to behave in the abbey. She started singing a song with very rude words.

The abbess knew what the words meant and she was very shocked that such rude words were being sung in the House of God. She decided on the severest punishment.

'We must wall this errant sister in. Let it be God who decides her fate.'

The nuns saw that at the side of the cellar there was already a small room just the right size for walling her into. The way into it was in need of repair, but there were some old bricks nearby. Jocunda was carried into the little room at the side of the cellar.

'*In dulci jubilo*, down, down, down we go,' she sang. She realised something serious was happening but she didn't understand what.

The nuns laid Jocunda on the floor and started mixing mortar. Soon they were bricking up the gap in the wall. The abbess wondered if she had been a bit harsh in her punishment. She sent to the kitchen for a fresh loaf of bread and a jug of water for Jocunda.

When Jocunda awoke from her drunken slumber she was in darkness and she didn't remember being walled in. She wasn't scared of the dark and she began to sing.

'*In dulci jubilo*, up, up, up we go.'

In St Leonard's Priory dinner was late. A few days earlier the prioress had died and she had just been buried. All of the nuns were very sad and they were also worried about who would be the next prioress. Their cellarer was late going to get their ale for dinner. When she went down the steps she was surprised to hear the sound of singing.

'Who's there?' she called out, but no one answered. Then the nun realised the singing was coming from the part of the cellar where they had walled up Jocunda the year before. She ran upstairs to tell the others and soon the cellar was full of nuns breaking down the brick wall. There was Jocunda! She looked just as well as the day they walled her in and the loaf of bread was still fresh and the jug of water had not been drunk.

'It's a miracle!' they all cried. 'We prayed to God and He heard our prayer!'

The nuns had missed Jocunda's beautiful singing and her jolly nature; they were delighted to have her back. They quickly realised that God had sent Jocunda back to be their new prioress.

Under Jocunda's leadership St Leonard's Priory became a much jollier place. There was better food, more wine and much more singing.

All of this time Jocunda's family had been very worried about her. When they discovered that she was now the prioress of St Leonard's they were amazed.

'However did that happen?' they asked her.

'By getting drunk and singing rude songs,' she told them. Her family didn't believe her, but they were very pleased that their naughty daughter, who had never liked doing what she was told, had become Prioress Jocunda.

When I first heard this story it was called 'Brother Jucundas' and was about a young man who became the prior of St Leonard's by getting drunk and singing. For centuries folk tales have had more stories about men and boys than about girls and women. This is partly because men and boys had more opportunities to do interesting things and partly because most storytellers were men. When I was a girl I normally dreamt of having the boy's part in stories because the boys did exciting things whilst the girls waited for something to happen.

Now that I am a writer I can decide who does what. I have given females more active and fun parts in my stories because I know lots of girls and women who have amazing lives doing exciting things. But, because this is a book of traditional stories, there are still more men and boys than there are girls and women. As you read on you might like to imagine how the stories would sound if the boys and girls were the other way around.

St Mary's and St Leonard's are real places in York. You can visit their ruins in York Museum Gardens. The area between them has never been excavated, but if archaeologists ever dig down I think they will find two cellars, separated by a bricked-up wall.

3

A Sweet History of Pontefract Cakes

Mr Hardwick liked to stride around Pontefract swinging his cane. One morning he strode into his classroom and saw a clown with a cane had been drawn on his blackboard. He knew the clown was meant to be him. He didn't think the clown looked much like him, but it wore a cravat just like he was wearing.

'Who drew this? Which of you useless boys did this?' he demanded.

The boys all stood behind their desks looking at the floor. None of them spoke, but Mr Hardwick heard sniggers from wherever he wasn't looking. Little George Dunhill had his eyes shut very tight so that he didn't cry. He had only just started school and was frightened of Mr Hardwick.

'I'm going to tell you something. Whoever drew this is going to get caned. I will cane his hand so hard that he will never be able to draw again and then I will cane his backside.'

None of the boys owned up or said who it was.

'I'm now going to tell you something else. If you are so useless that you will not tell me who did this, you are *all* going to get caned.' For half an hour he strode around the classroom swishing his cane in the air and using it to point at boys.

'Was it you?'

'No, sir,' they each said.

Mr Hardwick decided to start his punishment by caning the oldest boy in the class. All of the boys winced every time his cane came down on the boy's hand. Suddenly there was a crack and the cane splintered into little pieces of wood which showered across the room. Mr Hardwick was so angry he could hardly speak; he stormed out of the class and wasn't seen again that day.

Little George Dunhill managed not to cry until he got home and told Ann, his big sister, about Mr Hardwick.

The cane had been Mr Hardwick's favourite possession. He felt it made him look distinguished and it was useful for disciplining naughty boys. He was upset about having to pay for a new one. It made him so angry he couldn't sit still and he set off from the schoolmaster's house for a long walk.

Mr Hardwick walked past the walls of Pontefract Priory and the priory gardens. As he walked he grabbed angrily at a straggly plant growing there and pulled it up.

'Those useless boys!' he muttered to himself. 'Useless. None of them will ever achieve anything.' He swished the whippy plant around in his hand. 'They need beating like this!' he muttered as he walked along, swishing the plant against tree trunks, 'and they need beating like this.' He brought the plant down on a rock.

The next day the boys were not well behaved because they thought Mr Hardwick didn't have a cane. When one of them was caught daydreaming, Mr Hardwick produced a long whippy plant from his bag and used it to whip the boy's hand. A strange scent, like fennel, filled the air.

That night it was very dark, there was just a fingernail moon in the sky. Mr Hardwick looked around to check he wasn't being watched then made his way back, to Pontefract Priory by quiet paths. The spade in the bag on his back rubbed against his shoulders.

He heard a shriek then, '*whooo whooo*' behind him and he screamed. He saw the shape of an owl flying from the shadow of the woods. Mr Hardwick didn't like owls.

Mr Hardwick moved slowly along the priory wall, he was feeling for more of the straggly plants. His spade made a scrunching sound as he dug deep into the soft earth and pulled up as many of the whippy plants as he could find.

Back at home Mr Hardwick placed the plants into a hole he had prepared in his back garden. He backfilled the hole with cool, damp earth. That night he went to bed happy.

Next morning the schoolmaster watered the plants before breakfast. He was pleased that he could now grow his own supply of whips to beat useless boys with.

Little George Dunhill didn't like school; he couldn't stop worrying about doing something wrong and being whipped.

'Big boys say t' whip 'urts more than t' cane did,' he told his sister Ann, bursting into tears again. 'Big boys say Mister grows 'em in 'is garden so he won't niver run out.'

Late that night, Ann sneaked out of their home, which was at the top of town next to the castle, and walked along quiet backstreets. Her stomach felt knotted up inside her, but she had set herself a task and was determined to complete it.

The schoolmaster's house was dark so Ann knew he had already gone to bed. Ann gently lifted the garden gate latch. She heard an owl call '*whooo whooo*' from somewhere nearby as she crept to the bed of whipping plants growing by the house.

Ann started to dig the plants up; they smelt like fennel. Then she heard the garden gate open and saw Mr Hardwick walk in swishing his new cane. She froze, then slowly slid back into the shadows. Just then, the owl called again: '*whooo whooo*'.

'Ah!' Mr Hardwick jumped in the air and screamed in fright. His cane fell from his arm.

Ann thought it was funny that Mr Hardwick was frightened of owls. She had to put one of the plants in her mouth and bite on it hard to stop herself from laughing aloud. She was frightened of him hearing her and even more frightened of him finding her. Sweetness filled her mouth and trickled around her teeth.

Mr Hardwick picked up his cane and went into his house muttering crossly. Ann saw lights go on in the schoolmaster's house and she didn't dare to move until they had all been turned off. As she waited she chewed on the sweet plant. It made her mouth feel warm and her stomach felt calm again.

Once Ann was sure that Mr Hardwick was asleep she carried all of the plants out of his garden. They were heavy and filled her arms. She had planned to dump them in the river, but the sweetness lingering in her mouth persuaded her to take them home.

Before long, the Dunhill family had a healthy crop of the whipping plants growing in their garden. A visitor, who knew about plants, told them that it was called liquorice. It was good for unsettled tummies and curing colds. Ann and George loved chewing the woody roots and they started sharing them with their school friends.

Mr Hardwick was very angry when he saw that his whipping plants had been stolen during the night. He was cross with the boys and told them they were useless but because he was using his new cane he didn't hit them so hard. He didn't want to break it. The schoolboys discovered that liquorice sticks were very good to bite on when they were being beaten. The sweet taste of liquorice filled their mouths and took their minds off the beatings.

The schoolboys learnt, from George, that Mr Hardwick didn't like owls. Soon Mr Hardwick started to hear owls calling outside his house every night. Before long, he decided that he didn't want to stay in Pontefract teaching useless boys for the rest of his life and he moved away.

George and Ann were popular with the children for supplying them with liquorice sticks. Their parents started to boil up the liquorice to release the flavour without having to chew. Soon they needed more space for growing liquorice and used the castle grounds next door. One day, when George was chewing a liquorice stick and nobody was looking, he licked his finger and then put it in the sugar bowl. The sugar crystals stuck to his damp finger.

As he licked them off they mixed with the liquorice taste in his mouth. He did it again and again.

When George's mother discovered him with his finger in the sugar bowl she was cross. He explained that he had come up with a new flavour and she should try it. The family all tried it. Soon they became very busy making sweets flavoured with liquorice and sweetened with sugar. Everyone wanted to buy them.

After that the whole family worked in the castle gardens growing liquorice, or in the factory making liquorice sweets. They called the sweets Pontefract Cakes. When the other schoolboys were old enough to start work, the Dunhill family provided jobs for all of them. They turned out to be very useful boys.

Mr Dunhill stamped a picture of the castle and a raven on all of the sweets. Ann and George said that it should be an owl

not a raven but when their parents asked them why they didn't explain. Ann and George always thought of the picture on the Pontefract Cakes as an owl but kept quiet about the trip to Mr Hardwick's garden.

You can still buy liquorice sticks and they are good to chew on, but Pontefract Cakes are far better.

4

Tales from the Spot Bottom Hops

The folk who lived on Gilstead Crags held dances on moonlit summer evenings. They were called the Spot Bottom Hops.

'Let's dance!' the young ones said.

The older ones sat on the bilberry bushes growing around the flat rocks where the youngsters danced. The ripe berries burst beneath them and stained their clothes. As they watched the dancers they told each other stories. They always began:

'I will tell you a tale of long ago when giants lived in these lands …'

The flowing music of the pipes and fiddles energised the dancers and relaxed those who chose to sit and listen. Although no one believed in giants, the stories permeated the way they lived. They listened until the sun rose and then they all quenched their thirst by drinking the morning dew.

There were two children, Orin and Faye. Orin was a little imp who was full of mischief; his neighbour, Faye, was quiet and thoughtful. Faye didn't mix much with other children, but she loved Orin. They liked to go exploring together in the valley below Gilstead Crags.

'Play up here where there is sunlight, it's healthier,' Faye's mother pleaded. She thought a lot about the old legends of giants in the valleys, but the other parents felt it was best to let the children go exploring. They believed they would soon grow out of it.

In the evenings the two children returned grubby but safe. Faye said very little about what they had done, but Orin was always full of stories about their adventures.

'So what have you two been up to today?' Orin's father asked.

'Well,' Orin told him, with a cheeky glint in his eye, 'we ran down into the valley and were flying along by the beck when we saw a giant as big as the marketplace. She was sitting on a willow tree. We both froze and stared at her. She wasn't doing anything that could have harmed us. We just stood there staring, she saw us and smiled and that was all she did. I haven't forgotten what you said about giants, but they are not scary. Just big, they are really, really big.'

Orin's father laughed, but his mother turned pale. She didn't want Orin to go back down into the valley, but he still went.

The following day Orin's father asked him if he had seen any more giants.

'She was on the bank of the beck looking out for us. When we found her we stood still in wonder at her size. She is as big as a dance hall. And she moved a little, but slowly, so we were not scared. She had beside her a giant book and some paints. She drew us in her book and showed it to us.'

Another night, Orin told his father that there were often two giants and he and Faye had spoken to them both. The giants said they had been warned that the Little Folk might cast a spell on them. They were called Frances and Elsie.

Orin's father roared with laughter at his son's tales and giants became their regular evening discussion. The stories Orin told grew more and more amazing.

Then Faye's father heard about Orin's stories.

'Tell me about the giants,' he demanded, but Faye would not. It angered him that Orin's father was being so well entertained and not him.

'Did you see the giants today?' he kept asking. 'What are they like?'

Faye didn't want to talk about giants.

Eventually she said, 'Lend me your camera and I will show you the giants.'

Faye's father had a new camera. They were a recent invention and few people had them. He wondered whether to trust her with it, but after some instruction on how to operate it, Faye set off with Orin and the camera. They returned an hour later.

That evening, Faye went into the dark room with her father to develop the photographic plate and there was a giant! Her father looked at the picture in disbelief. It showed a girl giant with a warm smile and beautiful braided hair sitting on a willow tree. Faye's father was impressed with his daughter for taking such a clever photograph.

'Is that a friend of yours?' he asked. 'Did you set her up right in front of the camera to make her look big?'

'Of course it's a friend,' Faye said. 'My friend Frances; she really is big.'

Faye's father embarrassed her by taking the photograph all around Gilstead Crags. He wanted to know who the girl pretending to be the giant really was. Everyone looked at the picture, but no one knew the girl. Most of the locals thought it a very clever prank, but a few, including Faye's mother, were convinced that there were giants living in the valley.

The photograph was forgotten about.

Three years later, Faye's mother and her friend went to a folklore lecture in Bradford about giants. Afterwards, the speaker overheard them discussing Faye's photograph.

'Please can I see this picture?' he begged.

A few days later he visited them and was staggered by the photograph. Before Faye's family knew what was happening, experts on giants and professionals in the field of photography were flying in from all directions to see the picture.

One said, 'I cannot help but think, in the absence of more detailed information, that the photograph of the giant is not everything it is claimed to be.'

But another said, 'They are the most interesting and wonderful results I have ever seen.'

They all met Orin and he told them all of the stories that he had told to his father years ago.

Before long, word of the picture and tales of the giants had spread far and wide and reached the ears of Doyle. Doyle was a famous man who had written many books. He published the picture of the giant in a popular magazine. Then he wrote a book called *The Coming of the Giants*. But by then, Orin and Faye had both grown up. Orin continued to talk to Doyle about his giant friends. His stories never changed.

The photograph became well known throughout the country. After a while, Faye refused to talk about the giants any more. Then, years later, she confessed that she had asked a passer-by to pose for the photograph, standing close to the camera so that she looked like a giant.

Orin always said his stories were all true. The only thing he changed was that, when people talked about the giants in the valley, he explained that the giants called the valley 'Cottingley'.

To this day, on moonlit summer evenings, there are Spot Bottom Hops on Gilstead Crags. Some people who go tell stories about the Cottingley Giants. There are other people who believe the Cottingley Giants were just a joke made up by two young children.

In 1917 two girls called Elsie Wright and Frances Griffiths took a number of photographs of fairies. They claimed to have seen them playing near a beck in Cottingley.

Sir Arthur Conan Doyle, the author of the Sherlock Holmes stories, believed in Spiritualism. He thought that it was possible to contact people who had died; he believed in fairies too. When he heard about the photographs of the Cottingley

Fairies he went to meet Elsie and Frances and then he wrote a book called *The Coming of the Fairies*.

Some people believed in the Cottingley fairies. Other people thought Sir Arthur Conan Doyle was a very silly man. They believed that the girls had made the stories up and taken photographs of paintings of fairies.

I wrote this story because I wondered how the fairies felt about what had happened.

5

The Tongue that Told the Truth

Abigail hated not being allowed outside the gates. She walked around and around and around the neat hedges and lawns surrounding the manor house.

'What are you doing?' she asked Tim, the page boy, as he strode across the garden.

'Your father has sent me to count t' logs.'

'Whatever for?' Abigail followed him into the barn where the air was full of dust and the smell of horses. 'Oh!' she exclaimed as she saw how small the pile of logs was. 'That won't last long.'

Abigail checked that no one else was in the barn then she let her hand touch the back of Tim's hands. Tim took her hands in his.

'I have to go,' he said. 'I have to report back to your father.'

The manor house was in a tiny village called Bradford. It had been a beautiful summer, but Abigail had not been allowed

out of the garden to enjoy it. Everyone was frightened of a monstrous wild boar which lived in the forest surrounding the village.

Most summers everyone went out blackberry picking. Then the table in the manor house was full of apple and blackberry pies with crisp pastry, and steaming summer puddings. This year blackberries had become a rarity. The villagers were too frightened to go out and the berries were going mouldy where they hung, uneaten, on the bushes.

Whenever the villagers had to venture away from their cottages they were on the alert for the snorting of the boar. The flap of a pigeon up in the branches of a tree was enough to scare them. They would race back to their cottage, slam the door behind them and listen to the beat of the boar's feet chasing them, only to realise it was the thudding of their own heart.

Three villagers had already been gored to death by the wild beast. Now that it had a taste for humans, and knew where they lived, it seemed unlikely that it would go away.

Abigail didn't mind not having blackberries, but she hadn't thought about not having wood. If they could not cut logs for their fires and collect sticks for kindling, the villagers might freeze to death in their cottages. So might her family in the manor house.

The Lord of the Manor was worried. He had been out hunting the boar with his men, thinking it would be good sport, but the spears they threw only scratched the boar's tough hide and enraged it. If their horses hadn't outrun it they might not have survived. The boar was far bigger than any they had seen or heard of.

After talking to his page about logs, the Lord of the Manor sat for a long time by a cold fireplace deep in thought. In the evening he explained to his daughter what they were going to do.

That night Abigail lay in her bed sobbing and sobbing into her feather pillow. Her father sat beside her trying to comfort her, but whenever he reached out to touch her she wriggled out from under his hand.

'Go away! I hate you!' she shouted.

'Abigail, Abigail, why can't you understand? I'm doing this for you. You are of age to marry and what better way to find you a good husband? Any man brave and skilled enough to kill the boar will be a good man to wed. Do you want to spend the rest of your life trapped here? Unless someone kills the boar you will never be safe to leave again. What can I offer as a reward that is better than my most precious daughter? You have no other suitors.'

Abigail sobbed all the more, but there was no point telling her father how she felt about Tim. The daughter of the Lord of the

Manor had to marry a knight at least, if not the son of another lord. She felt she was more like a bribe than a bride.

During the following week, Tim was kept busy attending to the needs of the valiant young men who rode up to the manor house and announced their intention to kill the wild boar. He had to stable their horses in the evening and assist them getting dressed for combat in the morning. He also had to listen to them talking.

'Hey, page, help me with this armour and pass me my sword. I'm going to have some sport with that wild boar today. I'll soon be riding home carrying its head under my arm. Then I'll be having sport tonight too. Do you think the lord's daughter is a bit of a wild one?'

Tim felt as if a grey mist was filling his brain; all happy thoughts were filtered through it and turned dull. He spoke little and tried to focus on the tasks he was given. Then, one afternoon, Abigail's chambermaid pushed a note into his hand as they passed in the corridor: *Come to my room at midnight. A.* Tim knew that if the knight who had recently ridden out into the forest killed the boar, there would be someone else in her room before midnight.

That evening, when the knight returned, barely saddled on his horse and with a leg wound, Tim smiled for the first time that week.

The stairs to Abigail's room, high up in the manor house, were thickly carpeted, but Tim took his boots off to be sure he didn't make a sound. Her door was ajar and the glow of a candle flame invited him in. Abigail closed the door behind him and threw her arms around him. Their embrace was sweet but brief.

'Listen carefully,' Abigail said. 'I have a plan but we have to act fast.'

Tim had worked fast, but he wasn't sure if he was at the right oak tree. The light of the moon barely penetrated the thick canopy of leaves. In the distance he could see a speck of light. He believed it was a candle burning in Abigail's window and it gave him courage. He smelt the boar; a ripe smell like manure, so he knew it was close. Leaning against the trunk of the oak tree he opened the bag Abigail had given to him and ate some food. Soon it would be light. He didn't feel brave enough to do what he had to do and he didn't know if he would be fast enough. He felt exhausted.

Soon after dawn the morning light was just bright enough for Tim to find the cave entrance. Turning to look at the manor house he saw Abigail's window. That reassured him that it was the right cave. Whilst Abigail had been refusing to leave her room she had nothing to do but look out of the window and had spotted the boar's lair. Now Tim could hear the wild boar's snores echoing around the walls of the cave.

Tim judged his distance carefully, backing off from the cave entrance but not too far. Before long, the boar shuffled about and then it roared as it woke. Tim almost ran away at the angry sound. Then the boar pottered out, stretched and squatted down outside its lair. It was twice the size of any Tim had seen before. It looked like a large sack of wheat with ears. Tim felt reassured; it looked too heavy to run fast and only had very small legs.

'Come out and fight me, you daft beast,' Tim shouted to get the attention of the boar. It looked around as if it wasn't clever enough to tell where the noise was coming from.

'Take that!' Tim yelled throwing stones at the boar, 'and that!'

The boar got up and ambled slowly towards Tim. Its tusks curled like scimitar blades, and it had teeth like spearheads, but it was very slow. Tim moved slowly too, backing away from the boar. It would take a little while to lead the boar to the trap, but everything was going to plan. Tim glanced behind him to check he was heading in the right direction. In that moment, the boar charged. Despite its slender legs it moved as fast as a racing dog. When Tim turned back the distance between them had halved. Before Tim's brain had decided what to do his legs had begun to run faster than they had ever run before. He heard the boar pounding behind him as they both charged through the woods.

Tim was so surprised at the boar's tremendous speed that he nearly forgot to look out for the trap he had set. Tim saw the layer of bracken suspended on sticks just as he felt the boar's hot breath on his back. He veered to the side of the hole he had spent the night digging and fell, smashing his arm against a tree trunk. The ground shook beneath him and then ...

When the world stopped spinning, Tim was in pain but all that he could hear was the early morning calls of a few birds. He opened his eyes. He could see the wild boar's behind sticking up out of the hole, its legs hung still and limp. Tim crawled painfully to the edge of the deep hole. The boar had fallen head-first into the trap, its neck was broken, it lay still with its tongue lolling out of its mouth.

Abigail! That was Tim's only thought; he must let Abigail know. He tried to stand, but the arm that had hit the tree was so painful he had to use the other arm to support it. He sat down again, feeling dizzy. He realised he needed to cut off the boar's head to prove to the Lord of the Manor what he had done.

Tim managed to stand and then climbed carefully down into the pit. The boar's neck was so thick his small knife couldn't cut through it and with his injured arm he wouldn't be able to carry such a large trophy home. Then, noticing the boar's tongue, he decided that would be evidence enough.

Soon Tim was limping home with the tongue in Abigail's bag and a beaming grin on his face.

That same morning, a knight had set off early for Bradford with the intention of killing the wild boar and claiming the prize. He became lost in the woodland but then discovered the infamous wild boar caught overnight in a trap. Leaping into the pit he chopped off the boar's head with one swipe of his sword and then set off for the manor house, believing the prize was his.

For the first time that week, Abigail had left her bedroom and was pacing up and down near the garden gate. She heard the drumming of hooves growing louder, then a knight appeared with his reins in one hand and the gigantic head of the wild boar under his other arm.

A stable boy saw the knight too. He opened the gate wide to let him in and then ran into the house to tell everybody the good news. Soon the stable yard was full of people congratulating the knight.

'Where is Abigail?' the Lord of the Manor asked, sending servants to her room to bring her down. They returned saying she was not there. Had they listened, they would have heard her weeping behind the garden hedge.

'Silence!' cried the lord, and everyone obeyed. 'I declare that this brave knight will have the hand of my daugh…'

'I'll hear nowt of that!' said another voice, loud and determined. 'He did not slay t'wild boar. I did.'

Everyone turned to stare; Tim the page boy was standing in the gateway. He looked exhausted and was using one arm to support his other arm and hold a bag.

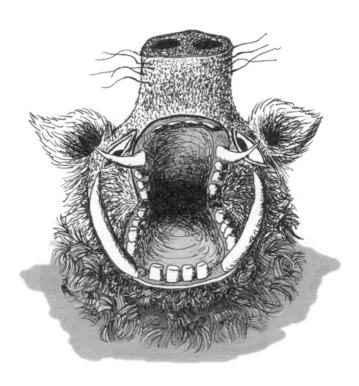

'Don't be ridiculous, carry on, my Lord,' shouted the knight.

Abigail stepped out from behind the hedge. 'Father, please listen to him.'

The Lord of the Manor stared from one to the other.

'Where is its tongue?' Tim asked, staring straight at the knight.

The knight was clearly baffled, he opened his mouth to speak, but his own tongue seemed unable to form any words.

'I couldn't cut off 'is whole head wi' my little knife,' Tim explained. 'So I just brought you this.' He opened the bag and the pink tongue fell out onto the ground at the lord's feet. Then Tim walked across to the boar's head and opened its mouth, and everyone saw that the tongue was missing.

The knight blushed; those few who were not congratulating Tim booed the knight as he mounted his horse and rode away. The Lord of the Manor had to accept that the young man who normally helped him to dress in the morning was to be his son-in-law. Seeing the joy on his daughter's face made it easier.

Soon Abigail and Tim were married and lived safely in the little village of Bradford without fear of the monstrous wild boar. They adored each other and by the example of their love and teamwork the little village became a town, and the town eventually became the big city that Bradford is today. Now no one in Bradford has to worry about being attacked by a monstrous wild boar, but if you look at the City of Bradford coat of arms, you will see that at the top is a wild boar's head, without a tongue.

6

The Upsall Crock of Gold

S unset coloured the sky gold.
An Upsall lad sat underneath an elder tree near Upsall Castle and looked at the beautiful sky. *If only I could reach up and tek some o' that gold*, he thought, *then I wouldn't 'ave t' sleep underneath this tree.*

The lad snuggled down in the leaves, pulled his coat around him and tried to sleep. Bats flitted out of the shadowy woods and an owl shrieked as it glided out of a barn. The night was cold and the lad felt he had hardly slept at all, but in the morning he could remember a dream.

He was standing on a bridge unlike any he had ever seen before. The river below him was far wider than those in the Yorkshire Moors, and the bridge was built up with houses and shops on it. Although he had never been to London he knew, in the way you do in dreams, that it was London Bridge. The dream was so clear in his head he almost felt it had happened. *How could*

a poor lad like me ever 'ave bin t' London?
he thought. *It must 'ave been juss a dream.*

That day the lad managed to get some work
on a farm digging potatoes. It was hard, but
in the evening he was paid with a big plate of
pudding and gravy and then a bowl of potato
and onion stew. He was also allowed to sleep
in the barn. It was warm in the hay.

The next morning he woke almost believing
that he had been to London and had stood
on London Bridge. The same dream again!
He knew it was unusual to have such clear
dreams and to dream the same thing twice,
but he had no time to think about it. He had
to get up and find some work.

It was a dreary day and few people
were about so the lad could find no work.
He used a little money to buy some bread
and then sat thinking about his life. He
couldn't see any way that an uneducated
young man, like himself, could ever improve
his circumstances.

That night he slept in a cave. It was damp and cold and hard. In the morning he woke up sore and stiff but certain that he had been to London and stood on the bridge. The same dream again!

All day the lad thought about the dream. By the evening he had made a decision: he would go to London and stand on the bridge. No one in Upsall would miss him and he was convinced that he was having the dream for a reason. He knew if he told anyone it would sound silly so he didn't tell a soul.

From Upsall to London Bridge is 222 miles. The young lad's journey was longer because he did not always take the best route. It took him six weeks to get to London. Some days he stopped to find work so that he had food.

Eventually he arrived at the River Thames in London. It was really wide and the bridge had buildings on it, just as he had dreamt. There were people herding animals across the bridge and lovely smells of food from street vendors. Rich men galloped across on horseback and poor men took their goods to market on squeaky old carts.

The Upsall lad was not used to so much activity. He walked confidently onto the bridge because it looked exactly like he had dreamt. He stood exactly where he stood in his dreams, looking down at the River Thames. He felt excited because he knew something important was going to happen. He also felt lonely. He realised he was hundreds of miles from anyone he knew. Before long he felt hungry. As the day passed he felt tired. Then he started to feel foolish; by the end of the day he felt really daft. He had walked 222 miles because of a stupid dream; now he was far from home, cold and hungry.

The lad was looking at one end of the bridge and then to the other, wondering which way he should go, when an old man walked up to him.

'Good evening,' he said. 'I've been over there selling fish and I've watched you standing here all day. Are you waiting for someone?'

So the Upsall lad told him about his dream.

'Strange things dreams are. I keep having a dream that there is a crock of gold underneath a big elder tree at Upsall Castle. I would follow my dream too, but I have no idea where Upsall Castle is.'

'Strange indeed!' said the lad. He decided it was time to set off home!

The lad's journey back from London was much quicker. He walked faster and stopped less to work. Arriving in Upsall one evening, he borrowed a spade, went straight to the big elder tree near Upsall Castle and began to dig. Before long, his spade clinked against something hard; an old crockery pot. He removed the lid and saw, in the moonlight, that it was full of gold coins. He soon had the pot out of the ground and his pockets full of gold.

After backfilling the hole, the lad slept right there under the tree, but he knew it would be the last time he ever had to sleep outside.

In the morning the lad took the pot and walked into the inn. He was able to order the best breakfast he had ever had ,and paid with a gold coin. As he was eating he looked at the pot lid. It had a strange pattern painted on it in square shapes with rounded edges.

The landlord said he thought the pattern was writing from another country.

'Why don't you hang it up here and see if anyone can read whar it says.'

The lad bought a house in Upsall and often took his meals at the inn. Whenever he met anyone in need of food and a place to sleep he took them to the inn and then back to his home to rest. As the years passed, he used up most of his gold coins and was thinking that his life might become difficult again. Then, one evening, when he was eating at the inn, the landlord beckoned him over. There was an old man at the bar.

'Where did you finding this pot?' he asked in a foreign accent.

'In a local field.'

'Are you knowing what it says? It's written in my language; in Hebrew.' The man was Jewish. He read it out to him: 'Look lower, where this stood is another twice as good.'

'What a strange message,' the Upsall man said (he was a young lad no longer). He pulled an expression that he hoped made him look puzzled.

That night, a few hours after dark, the Upsall man went back to the elder tree near Upsall Castle. He re-dug the hole, going much deeper than before. Eventually his spade clanked against something hard. This time he found a huge wooden chest so full of gold that it took him the rest of the night to dig it out and carry it all home. He knew it was the last work he would ever have to do.

The Upsall man continued to have an easy life but never became lazy. He spent most of his time helping other people who were in need and he always advised everyone he met to follow their dreams.

7

Robin of Loxley and the Pancake Surprise

R obin and Marion lay on a branch. The cold March air rippled inside their tunics.

'I think I can 'ear her,' Robin whispered.

Robin's mother had promised to be back on Shrove Tuesday. Robin couldn't help grinning at the thought. The children had decided to ambush her and both had pockets full of leaves and primroses to drop as she passed underneath them.

'Thas not thi mother,' Marion whispered back. 'Unless she spent t'week at your aunt's farm buyin' pans!'

Robin listened. *Tink, tink, chink, chink.* Before long a pedlar appeared in the lane. He only had three ponies; they were fat with bundles and bags and one also had saucepans tied on at both sides. The pans knocked against each other and chimed as the ponies clip-clopped along the path through Loxley Common.

The children watched the pedlar. He stopped beneath them and looked up and

down the lane. Then he sat down with a sigh on a large stone and pushed his hood down. They were amazed to see that he had well dressed hair and smooth skin like a rich man's. Robin and Marion lay very still.

The pedlar unstrapped a bag from the side of a pony and took out a bottle of wine and a silver goblet. Robin nearly fell off the branch with surprise. *He's not really a pedlar,* he thought. Robin and Marion watched him drinking his wine and eating some fine food. Their eyes explored the bags on the ponies then they glanced at each other.

After a while, the man repacked his bags and set off again. Robin's leg had gone to sleep through lying still so long. He had to kick it against the tree trunk until he felt life fizzing back into it, before he was able to jump down. He wanted to know what else the man had in his bags and why he was travelling in disguise.

"E might be one o' sheriff's men wi' tax money,' Marion said.

'Ey! And he dun want t' lose owt t' robbers.'

Everyone hated the Sheriff of Nottingham's men. If they were caught on their own carrying money they wouldn't be safe.

'Let's meet him at t' bridge,' Robin said, and the two of them hatched a plot as they sped down into Loxley Valley by a quicker route. They knew they could get to the packhorse bridge before the man in disguise arrived there.

A little while later the disguised man reached the bridge at the bottom of the valley. It was the only bridge across the River Loxley. He was hoping to get to the hunting lodge at Stanage before sunset and he led his ponies onto the bridge.

'YOU HAVE NOT PAID!' a loud voice boomed at him.

The man shrieked. It seemed as if the bridge itself was talking to him. He shook his head in disbelief and stepped back off the bridge. *Must have been thunder,* he thought, looking up at the sky, but it was a bright and clear day. The man stepped onto the bridge again.

'YOU HAVE NOT PAID!' The voice was louder this time and so he leaped straight off the bridge again.

The third time he tried to step onto the bridge his ponies refused even to go near it. The disguised man thought the bridge must be cursed and felt his breathing getting faster, he worried about what to do. He thought he would have to go a very long way round, either up-stream or down-steam, to find a safer place to cross.

Just then a young lad came down the path on the other side of the bridge.

'Ay up,' said Robin, greeting the disguised man as he greeted everyone. Then he threw a pebble into the stream and crossed the bridge without a care in the world.

The pedlar stared at him in amazement.

'Please, come back, stop!' he called after Robin. 'How did you get safely across the bridge?'

Robin turned around with a look of surprise on his face. 'I threw a coin t' ogre of course. He'll take nowt but best tha's got. Now tha's woke 'im up he'll be after thee if tha don't.'

At this the pedlar hastily undid one of his bags and threw it into the river. Then he carefully put a foot onto the bridge and edged forward. No voice called out to him.

He tugged at the ponies' reins and they followed him across the bridge. Then he hurried away as fast as he could go, relieved that someone had told him what to do.

Marion waited a little while under the echoey bridge before climbing up the riverbank with a wet bag. She could feel that it had coins inside it. When Robin came back they laughed and laughed.

Before long, there was someone else coming along the lane. It was Robin's mother! He was really pleased to see her and so Marion decided to leave them together. Before she left she handed Robin the bag of coins.

Robin and his mother went to their cottage just along the lane from the packhorse bridge. Soon they had the fire lit, the oven warming and the kettle on. His mother opened up her bags. She had bought some green woollen cloth from Barnsley market to make new clothes for Robin.

'Tis Lincoln Green,' she explained. 'I chose it for thee, knowing how tha likes t' hid in trees.'

Robin was delighted. He was also pleased that his mother had brought home a small joint of beef from his aunt's farm. Since the Sheriff of Nottingham had put their taxes up they didn't often have meat to eat. As soon as the oven was hot they put the beef in to roast and made some pancake batter. It was Shrove Tuesday, when everyone made pancakes before Lent began.

As the beef cooked, the smell filled every part of their little home. Robin's stomach made noises like the ogre under the bridge. They were about to start making pancakes when they both jumped. Someone was hammering on their door and shouting. That was not the sound of friends coming to visit! Robin's mother answered the door. Robin remembered that he had a bag of coins in his pocket. He hadn't exactly stolen it, but he thought it might be something to do with the visitors.

Frightened of being found with the coins in his pocket he hid them in the bowl of batter mix. As four soldiers marched into the room he placed the bowl in the bottom of the oven.

'Are you the scoundrel who stole money from an innocent man crossing the packhorse bridge today?' they demanded, grabbing Robin roughly by his tunic and searching his pockets.

'No sir, I stole nothing sir.'

'Well a gang of brutal thieves set on one t'sheriffs men here t'day and we won't rest till we find out who it was and get t'money back.'

They turned out the bag Robin's mother had brought back from Barnsley but found nothing to interest them there. Then they emptied all of the cupboards onto the floor. They kicked everything, including Robin when he got in their way.

'What's tha' smell?' one of the soldiers asked suddenly.

They all turned to the oven and opened the door. Robin wondered whether to run before they found the coins, but one of the soldiers was blocking the door.

'Smells like you have something good in here.'

The soldiers sat at the table and ate their roast beef whilst Robin and his mother waited on them. They had to provide plates and knives and drinks. Once the beef had all been consumed they left the cottage. One of them burped in Robin's mother's face as they marched out, leaving the door open.

Robin's mother sat down by the fireside and cried. She was tired from her long journey, hungry, and frightened by the soldiers.

'Tha didn't steal did tha?' she asked Robin.

He decided to tell her the story of the man disguised as a pedlar. It made her laugh. "'E must 'ave told them a different tale to not look like a daft wassock,' she said.

They were both hungry and a smell coming from the oven was making it worse. Robin pulled out the bowl of batter mixture, which had puffed up and turned golden brown. It was covered in beef dripping from the joint and smelt nearly as good as the beef. Robin tipped it out onto the table to cool. Then he started to break it open so that he could get the coins out. He was so hungry he started to eat the baked batter mix. It was hot and crispy and delicious! Soon his mother was also eating and then all that was left was a few crumbs on the table and a pile of coins.

' What'll tha do wi' them?' his mother asked.

That was what Robin was thinking about when he went to bed that night.

The next day Robin and Marion walked along the Loxley Valley and then up to Loxley Common. They visited local people, gave them a coin each and told them it was a gift from the Sheriff of Nottingham. Everyone asked them where the money had come from and so they told them about the ogre under the packhorse bridge.

By the end of the day Robin's sides ached from laughing at the story so many times. He decided that taking money from the rich and giving it back to the poor was the best thing he had ever done and he went home very happy.

Robin's mother had spent the whole day sewing new clothes for him. He tried on his new Lincoln green tunic and pulled the large hood up and over his face. He loved feeling that he was hidden inside it.

'T'is reet grand,' Robin said.

That evening Robin wondered if there were other ways that he could trick the Sheriff's men out of the tax money they carried. He felt warm in his new clothes and the big hood gently tickled his cheeks. Robin started to make plans. He realised that having a green tunic would be good for hiding in the woods and that might be very useful.

Yorkshire puddings are made with the same ingredients as pancakes but are baked in the oven. They used to be put underneath the beef joint so that they were flavoured by the juices dripping off the meat as it roasted. The word *pudding* used to mean a meat dish (like black pudding) although nowadays it normally means a dessert.

Yorkshire pudding was made by poor Yorkshire people and eaten before the meat. This was so that they started to fill up before they got to the most expensive part of the dinner and so would eat less of it.

I have searched in lots of books and archives to try and discover how Yorkshire puddings were invented. I have also tried to find out about Robin Hood's early life. All I have uncovered is that he was born in Loxley on the edge of Sheffield, which is why some people still call him *Robin of Loxley*. I tried to imagine what his childhood must have been like and by doing that I worked out how Yorkshire pudding might have been invented too!

Yorkshire Pudding

This is a recipe for traditional Yorkshire pudding. It will only work if you have a very hot baking dish in a very hot oven. Ask a grown-up to get the dish in and out of the oven for you.

Ingredients

200g plain flour
3 eggs
300ml milk
Sunflower oil or lard for the tin

1. Heat the oven to 230°C, 210°C for a fan oven, or gas mark 8.
2. Put the flour, eggs and milk into a bowl and whisk them together.
3. If you can wait for a few hours leave the batter to rest – it will make a better pudding.
4. Forty minutes before you want to eat, spread a little vegetable oil or dripping around a roasting dish and put it in the hot oven.
5. After ten minutes take the dish out and pour the batter mixture into it. Put the dish back in the oven and cook for half an hour.

6. When the pudding is well risen and golden brown, cut into squares and serve with gravy.

8

The Penhill Giant

Dahlia lay on a grassy bank in Wensleydale.

She watched the clouds. They looked as white and soft as the cheese she made. She lifted her head to check her flock of sheep. Soon she would lead them home, milk them and spend the evening making more cheese.

'Twenty-one, twenty-two, twenty-three.' That evening Dahlia counted her flock back in their fold in Carperby: 'twenty-four, twenty-five …'

'Twenty-six, twenty-eight, thirty.' Penhill, the giant who lived on Penhill, counted his pigs. Every day, Penhill made his pig-herds walk them past his window in pairs. He sat inside his castle and counted them because he didn't trust the pig-herds not to lose any.

His pigs were long white Yorkshire pigs, shaped like sausages on trotters. He thought about eating them and licked his lips.

Taylor was the chief pig-herd. He enjoyed looking after pigs, but it was hard work and Penhill never thanked him for what he did. He also had to collect peat for the fires, grow fodder and make up bales of straw for the pigs to sleep on in the winter.

Penhill sat in his big chair by the fireplace inside his castle. He was counting pigs. With one hand he stroked the whiskers on his chin and with the other he stroked the ears of Wolfhead, his boarhound. Both of his eyes were looking through the window.

'Two hundred and thirty-six, two hundred and thirty-eight, two hundred and forty.' Penhill was pleased that every pig was back in the castle grounds for the night. All evening he sat before his fireside with Wolfhead at his feet. Wolfhead was tired from a day spent in the dale watching over pigs and rounding them up in the evening. When Penhill laid in bed he imagined that his pigs were walking past his window *two, four, six, eight* ... soon he was fast asleep.

One day as Dahlia was watching her sheep she heard **thump, thump, thump, thump** coming down the dale. She realised it was Penhill and called her sheep to her.

'Purl, Knit, Bobble, Pom-Pom, Warp and Weft – come quickly, the giant is near.'

Suddenly the sky darkened. Penhill was standing in front of the sun. Wolfhead his boarhound was by his side. The boarhound's eyes were focused on the sheep. Its tongue was licking its lips. Then the giant spoke.

'Fee! Fi! Fo! Fum!
Local sheep are really dumb.
Wolfhead you are looking thinner,
Find yourself a sheep for dinner.'

As he said this he gave Wolfhead a kick and sent him running towards the sheep. Dahlia stood in front of her sheep with her hands on her hips.

'Oh no you don't!' she shouted. She had no idea how to stop Wolfhead, but she was not going to let him eat her sheep.

Seeing her standing there defiantly made Penhill angry.

'Fi! Fo! Fum! Fee!
How dare a girl stand up to me?
Dog leave those sheep, and for your snack
Eat up that girl –
Attack! Attack!'

Dahlia was used to dogs. She had grown up around sheep dogs.

'SIT!' she commanded as Wolfhead hurled himself towards her throat. The dog had learnt very early in life that if he didn't obey he got kicked. As he was in mid-air he heard the command to sit, so he sat. Right on top of Dahlia.

'Good dog,' she said in a hoarse whisper as she lay on the ground with the huge dog on top of her.

She could hardly breathe. She managed to pat the ground with her hand and whisper '*sit*' again. He obediently got off her chest and sat beside her. Dahlia lay in the grass listening to the **thump, thump, thump, thump** of the giant walking away. He had seen his dog leap then turned back to his castle without waiting to watch Wolfhound eat Dahlia.

'Here's my snap,' Dahlia said. She had packed up Wensleydale cheese sandwiches for her lunch. She offered them to the hungry dog.

'Good boy, good dog.,' she praised him and stroked him fondly as he ate her lunch.

'Two hundred and thirty-six, two hundred and thirty-eight, two hundred and ... and ... WHY ARE THERE ONLY TWO HUNDRED AND THIRTY-NINE PIGS?' the giant roared. It was evening. The pig-herds had been caring for the pigs since dawn. Then Wolfhead had rounded up the pigs and they brought them to the castle window for counting.

Penhill made the pig-herds walk all of the pigs back past his window again. There were still only two hundred and thirty-nine. He opened the castle door and kicked his dog out.

'Fee! Fum! Fi! Fo!
You dullard dog –
Back out you go!
Stupid, foolish boarhound dog,
Now go and find my missing hog.'

Wolfhead did not return that night, but in the morning he came home walking backwards. He had a pig's trotter in his mouth and he was pulling a whole pig along behind him. Quivering in the pig's heart was an arrow. Blood had run down the long white side of the pig like streaks in bacon. When Penhill saw that someone has shot one of his precious pigs he was enraged.

'Po! Pum! People Pie!
Whoever killed my pig must die!
Get every man in Wensleydale
And I will make the killer wail.'

The pig-herds sent out messages up and down the dale to tell all of the village men that they must come and stand on the cliff top because Penhill wanted to talk to them. The Wensleydale villagers were frightened. Whenever the giant got angry bad things happened, but they knew that if they didn't do what he demanded it would only make him worse.

The men assembled on top of the cliff and Penhill the Giant marched up with his bow on his back. It was made from a tree trunk. He looked all of the men in the eye and demanded to know which one of them had killed his pig.

'Not me sir!'

'Not me!' they all said.

That made the giant madder and madder.

'Se! Si! So! Sum!

I will slaughter all your sons.

Come tomorrow with all your kids

And I will find who shot my pig!'

Penhill shouted, then he stormed back to his castle.

Wolfhead knew his master was upset and stayed close by his side to try and comfort him, but Penhill kicked him out of his way. Wolfhead ran off, so Penhill called him back. He called and called, but Wolfhead did not obey him. Taking his bow from his back Penhill shot Wolfhead then returned to his castle alone.

At dawn the next day all of the men were standing on the cliff. Some of them were carrying babies and many had children with them. Penhill picked up his axe and was about to leave his castle when Taylor, his most trusted servant, spoke to him.

'Please sir, I have seen thirteen ravens and I believe it is a bad omen. Please have mercy on these village people or I'm certain something bad will happen to you.'

Penhill was missing kicking his dog and so he kicked Taylor instead. Once Taylor had recovered enough to get up he went to get some straw and peat.

The families on the cliff heard **thump, thump, thump, thump** and they knew that the giant was coming, but then the sound stopped. Penhill had not gone far from his house when he saw another dead pig lying on his path. This pig also had an arrow through its heart. **Thump, thump, thump, thump** then he stopped again. There were two more dead pigs. As the giant walked out to the cliff he found nine dead pigs. Every pig made him angrier and angrier. When he got to the cliff he was shaking with rage.

'Fi! Fi! Fo! Fax!
I'll kill you all with this big axe.
I'll not stop till you all are dead,
Your blood will make this cliff turn red.'

The villagers on the cliff were looking at the big shiny axe. Reflected in the axe they saw red light. They looked up to see where it was coming from. The giant's castle was on fire. Taylor was not prepared to work for the giant anymore. He had filled the castle with straw and peat and set fire to it. Flames were filling the windows like red curtains flapping in the breeze.

The giant noticed everyone on the cliff was looking in the same direction and he turned to see what they were looking at. Then he heard the very familiar bark

of a very familiar dog. He turned back
to see Dahlia walking onto the cliff top
with a bow across her back and Wolfhead
limping at her side. When Wolfhead saw
Penhill he leapt from the cliff top and dived
towards the giant. Penhill was so surprised
he lost his balance and fell over backwards.
His head crashed onto a large rock. The
thud of the fall brought down much of the
burning castle. The villagers started to run;
the giant was going to be furious.

'I think he is dead,' a child said.

Everyone stopped running and looked.

The only movement was Wolfhead limping away from Penhill the Giant and going back to Dahlia.

It was weeks before the smoke from the castle cleared. Then it became a place where children played in the ruins when they were out in the dale watching the sheep and they had had enough of imagining shapes in the clouds.

Nowadays there is no sign that either Penhill or his castle were ever there, but the top of Penhill, where his castle stood, is very flat and perfect for grazing sheep.

9

The Small-Toothed Dog

L ong ago there was a man called Sidney Oldall Addy. He lived in Norton which is now part of Sheffield; he loved old stories. Addy asked the oldest people he could find to tell him the stories their grandparents had told to them. He collected these old stories and published them in a book called *Household Tales with other Traditional Remains*. The next two stories are from his book and he heard them both in Yorkshire.

Once upon a time there was a merchant's daughter who waited for her father.

The daughter often had to wait a long time, but eventually her father always returned to their cottage in Sheffield. He brought back wonderful things: sapphire silks as smooth as still water, spices which held the smell of sunshine, and sticky honeycomb as sweet as love.

He traded some of his goods with local Sheffield men; some he kept for himself and some were gifts for his daughter. Although she missed her father when he went away she trusted he would always return. Over the years he came home to find his baby had become an infant, his infant had become a child and then his child had become a young woman. Each time he came back she was more beautiful and more loving than before.

But on one of his journeys, at dusk, thieves attacked him, knocked him on the head from behind and tore his baggage from him. They would have taken both his life and his goods if a dog had not come to his rescue. It was a large dog with an angry bark but tiny teeth. The dog snarled and ripped as he barked and bit the thieves until he had driven them all away.

When the thieves had gone, the dog took the merchant to his home, which was not a kennel but a handsome house. He dressed the merchant's wounds and nursed him tenderly until he was well.

Soon the merchant was ready to continue his journey home. Before starting out he told the dog how grateful he was for his kindness and asked him what reward he could offer in return. He said he would not refuse to give him the most precious thing that he had, and he had many wonderful possessions from all his foreign travels.

And so the merchant said to the dog,

'Will you accept a fish that can speak twelve languages?'

'No,' said the dog, 'I will not.'

'Or a goose that lays golden eggs?'

'No,' said the dog, 'I will not.'

'Or a mirror in which you can see what everybody is thinking?'

'No,' said the dog, 'I will not.'

'Then what will you have?' said the merchant.

'I will have none of these presents; I will have your daughter to live here with me in my house.'

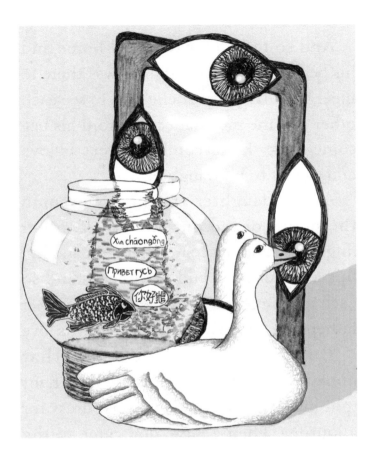

When the merchant heard this he was grieved, but what he had promised had to be done, so he said to the dog, 'You can come and fetch my daughter after I have been at home for a week.'

And so the father returned home and his beautiful, loving daughter was there to meet him. They were delighted to see each other and the merchant took from his bag some sticky honeycomb as sweet as love and gave it to his daughter.

As his daughter ate the honeycomb the honey oozed out and stuck to her fingers. The honey coated her chin and her lips and her nose and her cheeks and so, each morning and each evening, when her father kissed her she tasted as sweet as love.

But that week ended and that honeycomb was eaten and the merchant told his daughter that she must dress for a journey. Then a large dog came to the house. It had an angry bark but tiny teeth. The dog snarled and ripped as he barked and bit when he came to the merchant's house to collect the merchant's daughter. The dog stayed outside the door and would not go in. The merchant's daughter did as her father told her, and went out of the house dressed for a journey. When the dog saw her he was pleased, and said, 'jump on my back, and I will take you away to my house.'

So the daughter climbed onto the dog's back, and away they went at a great pace until they reached the dog's house many miles away. The daughter had never been so far from home and was anxious.

She tried to like living with the dog and to make herself at home, but she did not feel at home and she did not like living with a dog. After a month she wailed and wept so much that the dog noticed.

'Why are you crying?' asked the dog.

'Because I want to go back to my father,' she said.

The dog said, 'If you promise me that you will not stay at home more than three days I will take you there for a visit, but first tell me, what do you call me?'

'A large dog with an angry bark and tiny teeth,' she said.

'Then,' said he, 'I will not let you go.'

But a week went by and she wailed and wept so the dog promised again to take her home.

'But first tell me what you call me.'

'Oh,' she said, 'your name is ...' and she tried to think of the best name she

could give him, and finally she said 'Sweet-as-a-Honeycomb.'

'Jump on my back,' he said, 'and I'll take you home.'

So he trotted away with the daughter on his back for forty miles. Then they came to a stile.

'What do you call me?' he asked her, before going over the stile.

Thinking that she was safe on her way, the daughter said, 'A large dog with an angry bark and tiny teeth.'

But when she said this the dog did not jump over the stile. He turned around and galloped back to his own house with the daughter still on his back.

Another week went by and she wailed and wept so the dog promised again to take her to her father's house. So the daughter got on the dog's back and they reached the first stile as before, and then the dog stopped and asked, 'What do you call me?'

'Sweet-as-a-Honeycomb,' she replied.

So the dog leaped over the stile, and they went on for twenty miles until they came to another stile.

'What do you call me?' asked the dog, with a wag of his tail.

She was thinking more of her father and her own home than of the dog, so she answered, 'A large dog with an angry bark and tiny teeth.'

Then the dog was in a great rage, and he turned about and galloped back to his own house as before.

Another week went by and the daughter wailed and wept so the dog promised again to take her back to her father's house. She climbed upon his back once more, and when they got to the first stile the dog said, 'What do you call me?'

'Sweet-as-a-Honeycomb,' she said.

So the dog jumped over the stile and away they went. The daughter made up her mind to say the most loving things she could think of until they reached her father's house.

When they got to the door of the merchant's house the dog said, 'What do you call me?'

Just at that moment the daughter forgot the loving things that she meant to say, and began: 'A large dog ...'

The dog began to turn. She was going to say 'with a large angry bark', but when she saw how aggrieved the dog looked and she remembered how good and patient he had been with her she said, 'Sweeter-much-much-sweeter-than-a-Honeycomb.'

When she had said this, the dog sat down and she slid off his back. She thought the dog would leave her there and go but he didn't. The dog stood up on his hind legs then used his forelegs to pull off his dog's head and toss it high in the air. His hairy coat dropped off, and there stood the handsomest young man, clad in fine clothes and with the finest and smallest teeth ever seen.

Both of them were delighted to be two humans and they opened the door together and rushed in to tell the merchant. And of course, they were married and each day their love for each other grew and grew until it was sweeter, much, much sweeter, than a honeycomb and they lived together happily ever after.

I think people used to tell stories like this to teach children that they should obey their parents. This one may have been meant for girls to help them to understand that it was important for them to accept the man they were told to marry. Do you think it is still important to have stories like this?

10

The Hen-Pecked Husband

This is a very short story from Addy's book. When I read it I wondered if the same thing would happen nowadays. Here are two versions, his original one *and a modern one*.

Once there was a poor husband who was ruled by his wife and she hen-pecked him.

Once there was a man who never bothered to learn how to load the dishwasher properly. His wife asked him not to put the plates in the rack where the pans are meant to go.

He decided to leave her and go to another country.

He decided to go to the pub.

The husband set out on his way and had not gone far when he came to a farmhouse beside the road. Just as he was passing by the cock crowed, 'cock-a-doodle-doo!' but he thought the bird said, 'Women are meant to rule!'

When the husband got to the pub he was pleased to see England were playing football on television. He didn't recognise any of the England players' names. He moved closer to look and realised that it was women who were playing football.

The husband went a few miles further and came to another farmhouse and a cock crowed again, 'cock-a-doodle-doo!' He thought the bird said 'I think the same too!'

The husband decided to read the newspaper. It was full of news about the Prime Minister, who is a woman.

Then said the husband, 'I will go back and live with my wife for I'm certain that women are the rulers of men.'

Then the husband went back home and said to his wife, 'So where are the plates meant to go in the dishwasher?'

And they lived happily ever after.

And they lived happily ever after.

11

Beggars Bridge

Agnes Richardson had a warm heart. If you got too near to her there was a risk that your brain might start to melt and you might say foolish things. She could melt people's hearts too.

Tom Ferris spent as much time as he could with Agnes. It made him feel as if his brain was melting and he often said things to her which other people would have thought foolish. It was foolish for a poor young man like Tom Ferris to love a rich young woman like Agnes.

Squire Richardson loved Agnes; she was his daughter. He loved her, but she didn't melt his brain and nothing melted his heart.

Agnes Richardson knew that she was happiest when she was with Tom.

Tom Ferris knew that he could hop across the stepping-stones in the River Esk at Glaisdale and visit Agnes. She met him on the moors on summer evenings and they watched the sunset together.

Squire Richardson knew that marrying the right kind of person was important. He planned to find a rich man and tell Agnes to marry him.

Agnes Richardson dreamt about Tom, although he was often far away from her at sea.

Tom Ferris dreamt about Agnes when he was far away from her at sea.

Squire Richardson did not dream. He slept soundly knowing he was right about everything.

Agnes Richardson knew that Tom always returned from his voyages. She was always looking out for him.

Tom Ferris knew that he could wade through the rushing waters of the River Esk to be with Agnes. He rolled up his trousers and carried his boots above his head to keep them dry. Then he and Agnes cuddled up together, out of the autumn winds, where her father could not see them.

They talked for hours and Tom told Agnes about his sea voyages and the love he felt for her.

Squire Richardson knew that love was a silly thing and could never make up for lack of money. He did not know that his daughter was meeting Tom Ferris.

Agnes Richardson worried about Tom trying to cross the River Esk in winter. The freezing waters charged down the valley like an angry father in a rage.

Tom worried about missing Agnes because he was only home from his ship for a few days. The icy waters thumped against his chest as he waded into the River Esk.

In winter, Agnes and Tom hid in the stable. Her smile warmed him and there was a little heat from the horses.

Squire Richardson worried about nothing. He knew he was right.

Agnes Richardson said, 'Yes.' She did want very much to marry Tom, but he must ask her father and she knew her father would not be pleased.

Tom Ferris said, 'Please may I have your daughter's hand in marriage?'

Squire Richardson said, 'No! No! No! No! No! I will never let my daughter marry a poor man like you. Who do you think you are coming in here with your dirty boots on my carpet. You are just a beggar, go away!'

Agnes Richardson was all that Tom wanted and he would have her on any terms.

Tom Ferris asked the squire, 'If I become as wealthy as you are, will you permit me to marry Agnes?'

Squire Richardson said, 'Yes, but until then you must not meet Agnes.'

Tom Ferris was delighted. Squire Richardson had said, 'Yes!' All he had to do was to become as rich as the squire. He had to tell Agnes the good news, but there had been a storm and the icy waters hurtling down the River Esk were so dangerous he dare not cross.

Sir Francis Drake sent a message to Tom to say that a Spanish Armada was sailing to England. He was setting sail the very next day and Tom had to be on board his ship.

Tom Ferris left without saying goodbye to Agnes Richardson, without being able to tell her the good news.

Sir Francis Drake said, 'We must fight the Spanish Armada.'

Tom Ferris said 'Yes, Sir!'

He worked hard and fought well. After he and Sir Francis Drake defeated the Spanish Armada he was paid, but it was not enough money for him to marry Agnes.

Sir Francis Drake said, 'You worked hard and fought well. Would you like to stay on my crew?'

Tom Ferris said 'Yes Sir!'

He sailed over many seas and travelled as far as the West Indies. Before long, he was captain of his own ship. Then, Tom Ferris captured a ship from some dangerous pirates. He sailed the pirate ship back to London where he sold it for a very big bag of money.

Tom Ferris bought some very smart clothes.

Tom Ferris paid for a coach to drive him all the way to Squire Richardson's house.

Tom Ferris still had the very big bag, almost full of money.

Squire Richardson was a little surprised when a handsome and rich young man appeared at his door. He was even more surprised when Tom told him who he was and reminded the squire of his promise.

Agnes Richardson was not at all surprised to see Tom. She had always believed that he loved her and that one day he would return.

Agnes Richardson was very, very, very happy.

Tom Ferris was very, very, very happy too.

Agnes Ferris and her husband, Tom, went to live in Hull. Tom did not go to sea again because he wanted to be with Agnes.

They ran a shipping company in Hull and continued to make lots of money. Eventually Tom became the Lord Mayor.

Mr and Mrs Ferris often went back to the Esk Valley to see the squire. One winter's day, Tom was by the River Esk watching the flood waters rushing down the valley. He remembered how he had felt when he couldn't cross the river to see Agnes. Tom decided to pay for a bridge to be built over the River Esk. If there are ever lovers living on separate side of the river again, he didn't want them to have to wade through icy water to be together.

The bridge is still there in Glaisdale and it is known locally as the Beggars Bridge, although some people think the Lovers Bridge is a better name for it.

12

The Silent Drummer Boy

Baby kicking
Inside his mum.
Drum, drum, drum, drum.
The baby's spoon
Hits everything,
Dong-ding, dong-ding.
He hears a tune,
He starts to hum,
Pom, pum, pom, pum,
Pom, pum, pom, pum.

Have you noticed how some people have natural rhythm? They seem to be born with it.

Once there was a baby boy who loved his rattle. *Rat-a-tat-a-tat-tat-tat* he shook it, *rat-a-tat-a-tat-tat-tat*, *rat-a-tat-a-tat-tat-tat*.

'Take that blessed rattle from the bairn,' the husband shouted at his wife.

Then the little boy started to swing his legs. *Kicky-kick-a-kick-kick, kicky-kick-a-kick-kick,* he kicked against the husband's seat, *kicky-kick-a-kick-kick.*

'Put him somewhere else,' the husband shouted. When he had agreed to take in an orphan boy he hadn't expected him to be so much bother.

One day the boy was given a tin of biscuits. Instead of eating them he banged the tin. That day the husband decided he would not have a foolish orphan boy growing up with his own children. The boy was given to the neighbour, Mrs Threakston. She was deaf.

The little boy loved Mrs Threakston. He also loved to watch the soldiers marching to and from Richmond Castle. Whatever rhythm their drummer beat, the little boy played it on his biscuit tin for days afterwards.

'My little drummer boy,' Mrs Threakston called him.

'Ay up, drummer boy,' the soldiers said when they saw him.

Then Mrs Threakston died. The boy was six. He went back to the family next door. That night the husband took ale with the drum major. He told him about a young child who was not overly fond of food but who had a passion for drumming. He explained that, for a certain fee, the boy could become his.

The soldiers in Richmond Castle felt insulted to have such a little child join them. But when the boy was given a drum and shown how to play, they had to admit he had talent. There was one soldier, Matthew, who made sure the others did not kick the boy too often or take all of his food.

'Tha looks grand,' Matthew said when the boy was given a uniform, 'nearly as smart as King Arthur and the Knights of the Round Table.'

'Who are they?' the boy asked.

Next day, Matthew and the boy were sitting on a large stone near the River Swale and Matthew told him a story...

Long ago there was a stone just like this one, but it was a magic stone.

In those days they needed magic because they didn't have a king. Uther Pendragon had died and no one was ruling the land. If the shoreline of England had come under attack there would have been no one to defend the country. The barons and knights had been squabbling and everyone was worried.

Now at this time, a tournament had been organised, a special event where knights practised their fighting. There were two brothers and Kay, the eldest, was getting ready to go.

'You had better pack your bag too,' their father said.

'Who, me?' Arthur asked.

He was too young to enter the tournament and he thought he would have to stay at home.

'Yes, you.'

On the first day of the tournament Kay was so excited that he set off from the inn where they were staying without his sword.

'You!' he called when he realised his mistake.

'Who, me?' Arthur asked in surprise. Kay didn't normally talk to him.

'I have left my sword at the inn. Go fast and get it.'

Arthur ran to the inn, but the door was locked because everyone was at the tournament. Racing back to tell his brother, he saw a bright light in a churchyard; it was the sun glinting off a sword stuck into a big stone (like this stone we are sitting on). Arthur couldn't believe his luck!

Arthur leapt onto the stone, grasped the sword by the hilt and slid it out. The sword quivered in his hand as if it was alive. He was so pleased he pretended to fight an invisible attacker before running back to Kay.

Kay's name had just been called for the single combat; a fight with swords. As Arthur arrived, Kay grabbed the sword from him and ran straight into the ring. Wherever Kay stood the sun reflected on his sword and he struck his opponent with every swing. Soon Kay had won his third match, but there was a disturbance in the crowd. People were all nudging each other and pointing at him.

'Where did you get that sword? Did you pull it from the stone?' the Marshal asked.

Whilst Kay had been waiting for Arthur he had heard that there was a sword stuck in a stone in the churchyard and a sign on it saying, *Whoever can pull the sword from this stone is the Once and Future King.* Many men said they had already tried but failed and Kay had decided he would try, too. Now he stared at the sword in his hands and saw how elegant it was. He looked at the crowd of people who were looking at him.

'Yes,' said Kay without any hesitation. 'I pulled it out.' He raised his head, he felt like a king.

Everyone gasped and some people bowed down before him.

'Did you really?' His father had stepped forward.

Kay could not look him in the eye.

'Come here,' the father called to Arthur.

'Who, me?'

'Did *you* pull this sword from the stone?'

Arthur nodded his head. He was feeling dizzy. He had just heard the story about the stone too. It had been easy to pull the sword from the stone, but he knew he wasn't the king. Some people were bowing down to him and some were shaking their heads.

An old man approached. He wore a blue-grey cloak which was white at the front with brown flecks. He had a short neck and a sharp nose. Arthur's father ran to him.

'Merlin, Merlin,' he cried as they hugged.

Arthur thought Merlin's nose would scratch his father's face.

'We have to tell you both something important,' his father said, leading the two boys into a striped tent on the tournament field.

Twenty minutes later Arthur felt even dizzier. Merlin and his father had explained that his father wasn't his father. Arthur had been born in a beach cave in Cornwall and his real father was King Uther Pendragon who had died years ago. Arthur had been king for most of his life and not known it!

'If the king's enemies had found out they would have killed you,' Merlin explained. 'Your parents were not married so your mother couldn't protect you. I took you away by boat and this family loved you as their own.' Merlin held his hand up to Arthur's father and brother.

The next thing Arthur knew he was being walked back to the churchyard and lifted onto the big stone. They passed him the sword. Arthur held it up and saw that the churchyard was full of people. He slid the sword back into the stone.

'Ooooh,' they all cried.

Then Arthur pulled it back out of the stone and held it high above his head.

'Hail the king! Hail the king!' everyone cried and knelt before him.

'Who, me?' Arthur asked in disbelief.

'Yes, you,' Merlin said, 'King Arthur, our Once and Future King.'

The people all bowed down again and in that moment Merlin turned into a blue-grey bird of prey. 'Kik, kik, ki, kik,' he called as he rose in the air and flew away.

When the people looked up again, Merlin had disappeared. Their new king had a glinting sword in his hand and a baffled look on his face.

The church clock chimed.

'Come on, we'd better get back for band practice,' Matthew said.

'But what happened to King Arthur, and who were the knights?'

'I'll tell you another day, I promise.'

After band practice the boy carried on drumming. All of his spare time was spent drumming, the soldiers were not always happy to hear his drumming, so they gave him jobs to do.

'Go to the store and ask for a long weight,' they said, trying not to laugh. The little boy stood in the store for hours, waiting.

Eventually the quartermaster said, 'You have had a long wait.'

'I've had nowt.'

'On your way lad, be gone.'

The boy worried that he would be in trouble for not returning with the long weight, but the soldiers laughed and were not cross.

Once, they sent him out at night to get a bucket of night air, from the middle of the woods, where it would be freshest. He didn't mind because he liked helping people.

If Matthew caught the other soldiers sending him on foolish tasks he stopped them. 'Come with me, lad, and I'll tell you more about King Arthur...'

After Arthur had been recognised as the king he arranged for all of the knights to meet him at Camelot, his father's palace. The hall was laid out with rows of tables, and one big throne by the fireplace for Arthur.

When the knights arrived they argued about who should sit at the top near Arthur and the fireplace. Arthur had no idea how to get them to behave.

'I wish we had one big round table with no top or bottom,' he muttered to himself.

Out of the corner of his eye he saw

a blue-grey bird dart in through an open window. The bird flew to him and transformed into Merlin.

'You've had a very good idea,' Merlin said.

'Who, me?'

There was a crack like a whip in the air and a puff of sparkling smoke. When it cleared there was a huge circular table with a seat for everyone. Now no one would ever be either at the top, or at the bottom, again.

'You must be a wizard!' Arthur said.

'Who, me?' Merlin said. He winked, turned into a bird and flew away.

From that moment on all of the knights accepted that King Arthur was a good ruler and very fair.

A few days later, King Arthur heard reports that a giant was causing problems. *Someone needs to sort him out,* he thought. Then he remembered, *I'm the King, it will have to be me!* The knights were all prepared to go with him even though they would be risking their lives.

'I'll take Sir Bedivere,' Arthur said.

The two of them set off on their steeds and galloped to the coast. The giant had captured a young woman and taken her to St Michael's Mount in Cornwall, so they borrowed a rowing boat and set off across the sea in a raging storm.

They arrived at the island tired and drenched, and heard more thunder. In the distance they saw a bright fire burning and headed towards it. The fire was in a cave entrance. Through the smoke they saw the giant asleep beside it. The thunder was his snores.

'Look! There's the girl,' Bedivere whispered. She was tied up in the cave.

'We might be able to slip past him and rescue her,' Arthur said. Their sodden clothes steamed as they got closer to the fire.

Inside the cave Arthur unsheathed a small knife, but the giant heard it and woke up. He knew someone had a weapon.

'Who's there?' the giant bellowed, rising to his feet.

Arthur and Bedivere froze, hoping he couldn't see them in the darkness of the cave.

'I can smell men,' the giant roared. His hand clasped an oak tree's trunk and the ground shook as he uprooted the tree.

Arthur and Bedivere cut the girl's ropes then drew their swords and looked at each other; she could see fear in her rescuers' eyes.

'I'm waiting for you,' the giant bellowed. He tore the roots and branches from the tree and swung it like a club in front of the cave's entrance.

'Next time it swings up …' Arthur said, and they both ran out of the cave. They were only able to prod their swords at the giant's knees before the club swung down and they retreated.

'Ha! Ha!' the giant roared, bending right down to look at them. 'You can't harm me.'

Arthur ran straight out to the giant's face, and struck one small blow above his eye then darted back before the giant could catch him.

'We will have to try something else,' Sir Bedivere said. The club was swiping past the cave mouth so close it created gusts of wind.

'Let's charge him,' Arthur said. Then he noticed that the giant was swinging his club slightly to the side of the cave entrance. By the light of the fire they could see that the blood from the cut on his forehead had run down into his eyes and with both hands on the club he couldn't wipe it away.

'We might be able to run past him unseen.'

The three of them ran out of the cave, and straight between the giant's legs. The giant heard them and was groping blindly in their direction. His hand found Sir Bedivere and he picked him up.

'Run! Save yourselves!' Sir Bedivere cried as his sword fell to the ground.

'This way,' Arthur called to the girl, but she had disappeared.

'Yarrrrrr!' The giant moaned in pain as he fell to his knees then crashed to the ground, releasing Sir Bedivere from his grip. Arthur and Sir Bedivere could see the hilt of Bedivere's sword sticking out of the giant's armpit, and they could see that the tip must be in his heart...but they didn't understand how it had got there.

'Come on, let's go,' the girl said, jumping down from a tree and beckoning to them to follow her.

Arthur and Sir Bedivere looked at each other in amazement, then they looked at the girl, then up at the tree as they realised what she had done.

'Thank you,' she called, running down the hill. 'You two were so daring and brave.'

'Who, us?' Arthur said. 'I think you are the daring and brave one.'

But Arthur was brave too and so were all the knights. They were always ready to help anyone in trouble, to make sure justice was done, and they were always polite. Those three things were known as The Code of Chivalry.

'Are there still knights now?' the boy asked.

'No there haven't been any for a long time,' Matthew explained. 'But people say they're not dead, they are sleeping with Arthur underneath Richmond Castle. Some people say that if the shoreline of England is ever attacked again they will wake up and defend us.'

'Do you think they will?'

'Come on, it's time to get back to the barracks.'

A few weeks later Matthew went on leave to see his family and the boy felt lonely. He was wandering aimlessly around the castle grounds when a group of soldiers spotted him.

'Ey, come here lad, we've a job for you.'

They were near the castle keep and had started digging the ground to build a new shed.

'Wha does tha think of this?' They showed him a hole in the ground between some rocks.

'Whas down there?'

'We don't know, laddy, but we wondered if you could fit down there and tell us. Folks 'av always said there is a secret passage from here t' Easby Abbey; an escape route in case of a siege.'

'How will we know where 'e ' as got to?' one of the soldiers asked.

'I could beat my drum,' the boy said, peering into the black hole. 'You would be able to hear me and follow above ground.'

They all agreed that was a good idea and before long the boy was wriggling down the hole and into the tunnel. There was space for him to stand, so he hung his drum around his neck and began to beat. **Bang.** *Bang,* the beat echoed back to him from the walls. He could tell from the sound which way the passage went. **Bang,** *Bang.* **Bang,** *Bang.*

Above ground the soldiers couldn't hear the echo, they only heard the beat – boom, boom, boom, through the earth. They followed the sound out of the castle gate.

'A tunnel right unda t' market place, who'd a thought that!'

'It can't go t' Easby Abbey, it goes north.'

'He's turning, it goes along river.'

'It is going to Easby!'

They followed the regular beat of the drum for a mile. Then it stopped.

'Do you think he's found summat?'

'Might be scratching his nose.'

'He'll start again in a minute.'

The drumming did not start again. Ever.

Some of the soldiers went back to the castle and called down into the hole but got no reply and they couldn't fit in themselves. Others waited by the river for the boy to drum again.

Eventually, they all went back to the barracks. When Matthew returned a few days later no one wanted to tell him what had happened but they knew they must. They took him down to the spot on the river where the drumming had stopped. It was near the big stone where Matthew used to sit and tell the boy stories. Together they heaved the stone until it was in the exact spot where the drumming had stopped and Matthew sat on the stone and he wept and wept and wept. The stone is still there and the path has become known as *The Drummer Boy Walk*.

Matthew thought a lot about his little friend, and he eventually realised what must have happened to him.

The brave little boy beat his drum in the dark. He felt that he could see the path by listening to the echo and he knew that he was helping his friends, he loved helping his friends. **Bang,** *bang,* **bang,** *bang* the echo was coming back louder, he could sense that he was entering an underground chamber.

'Are the shores of England under attack?' The boy jumped. 'Who said that?' He froze with his drumsticks in the air.

The boy heard the sound of a sword being unsheathed. Then he saw it, a beautiful sword glimmering with light. A man in armour held it up and shadows danced around the room between sleeping men.

'I said that. I am Sir Bedivere and I ask you again; are our shores under attack?'

A few of the men were rubbing their eyes and sitting up.

The boy shook his head.

'Then you must not disturb King Arthur.'

'You already have.'

The man on the largest bed sat up and put a crown on. 'Are you alone?'

'Yes, Sir, mi friends wanted t' know where t' passage went Sir and I'm beating mi drum so they can 'ear me above, Sir.'

'Then you are a very brave boy, ready to help, polite too. You would make an excellent knight and we could use a good drummer. Would you like to join us?'

'Who, me?'

'Yes, you. I would like you to join us, but you must stop drumming.'

The chamber became dark again and the only sound was men breathing.

Arthur and his knights are still there, waiting for the time when they have to defend England again. Lying in the cushion of Arthur's arm is a sleeping boy. There is a rosy glow on his cheek, a smile on his face and a drum and two drumsticks are waiting at his side.

13

The Explicit Fabula

In South Yorkshire, when a storyteller had finished, they used to say:

> My tale's ended,
> T' door sneck's bended,
> I went into t' garden
> For a bit of thyme.
> I've telled my tale,
> Now thee tell thine.

It means you have read this book and these stories have been clearly told to you. Now your life as a storyteller can begin ...

Society *for*
Storytelling

Since 1993, the Society for Storytelling has championed the art of oral storytelling and the benefits it can provide – such as improving memory more than rote learning, promoting healing by stimulating the release of neuropeptides, or simply great entertainment! Storytellers, enthusiasts and academics support and are supported by this registered charity to ensure the art is nurtured and developed throughout the UK.

Many activities of the Society are available to all, such as locating storytellers on the Society website, taking part in our annual National Storytelling Week at the start of every February, purchasing our quarterly magazine *Storylines*, or attending our Annual Gathering – a chance to revel in engaging performances, inspiring workshops, and the company of like-minded people.

You can also become a member of the Society to support the work we do. In return, you receive free access to *Storylines*, discounted tickets to the Annual Gathering and other story-telling events, the opportunity to join our mentorship scheme for new storytellers, and more. Among our great deals for members is a 30% discount off titles in the *Folk Tales* series from The History Press website.

For more information, including how to join, please visit

www.sfs.org.uk